MORE THAN TWO ESSENTIALS
POLYAMORY AND JEALOUSY

Eve Rickert and Franklin Veaux

Polyamory and Jealousy
A More Than Two Essentials Guide

Text copyright ©2015 by Eve Rickert and Franklin Veaux
All rights reserved. No part of this book may be used or reproduced in any manner whatsoever without written permission from the publisher except in the case of brief quotations in critical articles and reviews.

Digital print edition v1.0

Thorntree Press, LLC
P.O. Box 301231
Portland, OR 97294
press@thorntreepress.com

Cover design by Amy Haagsma based on cover
illustration © Paul J Mendoza 2014
Interior design by Jeff Werner
Copy-editing by Roma Ilnyckyj

ISBN 978-1-952125-23-2

Library of Congress Cataloging-in-Publication Data
Names: Rickert, Eve, author. | Veaux, Franklin, author.
Title: Polyamory and jealousy / Eve Rickert and Franklin Veaux.
Description: Digitial print editIon V.1.0. | Portland, OR : Thorntree Press, [2022] | Series: More than two essentials | Includes bibliographical references. | Summary: "Eve Rickert and Franklin Veaux, authors of More Than Two: A Practical Guide to Ethical Polyamory, present Polyamory and Jealousy, part of the More Than Two Essentials series. The essentials take sections from More Than Two, expand on them, and present them in a practical, easy-to-use format that can be read in a single sitting. In this booklet, you will find pragmatic ways to handle feelings of jealousy when they arise. You'll learn tools for identifying jealousy, strategies for decoding what it means, and hands-on advice for dealing with it before it undermines your relationship"-- Provided by publisher.
Identifiers: LCCN 2022000980 | ISBN 9781952125232 (paperback)
Subjects: LCSH: Non-monogamous relationships. | Jealousy. | Sexual ethics.
Classification: LCC HQ980 .R53 2022 | DDC 306.84/23--dc23/eng/20220315
LC record available at https://lccn.loc.gov/2022000980

*The worst thing about jealousy is
how low it makes you reach.*

ERICA JONG

IT'S BEEN JUST OVER A YEAR since the official publication of *More Than Two: A Practical Guide to Ethical Polyamory*, our 500-page manual on the ethics, emotions and practicalities of plural relationships. In that time, the book has sold about 20,000 copies, and we've heard dozens of stories of the personal and relationship transformations it's brought about. We're amazed, humbled and more than a little stunned by the overwhelming response to the book.

But we wanted to reach more people than just those who feel up for a 500-page deep dive. Although we designed *More Than Two* as a reference book, so you could jump straight in to the chapters you need most, we wanted a way to give people what they need in a more bite-sized format—as well as an easy entry point into the book. And so *More Than Two Essentials* was conceived. The idea: Release key chapters from *More Than Two*, revised and with new material, focused on particular problem areas. The obvious topic to start with was jealousy.

We've learned a lot in the past year, talking to hundreds of people at conferences and on our book tour. We've learned about some things we left out, and some things we got wrong. This booklet is adapted from chapter 8 of *More Than Two*, but we've trimmed and added, revised and reworded, and tried to make the chapter even more relatable to a wider range of people. The most important change is that we try to speak more directly to the at-times overwhelming emotional experience of jealousy—and to the fact that people who experience it are not alone—and attempt to separate the need for self-care, support and reassurance during the jealous experience from the cognitive work and communication that needs to come after.

We hope this work helps you on your journey.

Eve Rickert and Franklin Veaux
Vancouver, BC and Portland, OR
December 2015

THE GREEN-EYED MONSTER

So you're in a polyamorous relationship; you're involved with someone who has another partner. There you are, cruising along, and *wham!* You see something, or hear something, or think about something, and now you're in the thick of it. Jealousy. It happens, sometimes when we least expect it. When it does, we can feel like we want to set fire to the world before running into a dark cave, screaming "I will never let anyone get close to me ever again!" (Or maybe that's just us.)

We give such talismanic power to jealousy that the fear of it alone can shape our relationships. We've never heard anyone say, "Polyamory? I wouldn't want to do that. What if I feel angry?" or "What if I feel sad?" But many people say, "Polyamory? What if I feel jealous?" The fact is, at some point you will. Few people are born immune to jealousy. The good news is, jealousy is just an emotion, like any other emotion. Sometimes you feel sad, sometimes you feel angry, but you don't let those feelings define you. They don't run your life. Jealousy doesn't need to either.

WHAT IS JEALOUSY?

Jealousy is the feeling we get when we drag tomorrow's rain cloud over today's sunshine. It's the feeling that we are about to lose something important to us, including maybe our self-worth, to someone else. It's the fear that we aren't good enough, that the people around us don't really love us, that everything is about to turn to ash. It comes like a thief in the night, stealing our joy. Jealousy is a sneaky thing. It sits behind us whispering that we are the victim, not the villain: that the people around us are wronging us, and we must act to protect ourselves. And perhaps most destructively, it tells us not to talk openly about the way we're feeling. It thrives on secrecy and silence. At its most toxic, it makes us angry at others and ashamed of ourselves at the same time.

Jealousy wears many faces because, unlike surprise or fear or anger, it is built of many emotions. Insecurity, fear of loss, territoriality, inadequacy, entitlement, poor self-esteem, fear of abandonment…all these can pile onto one another to make different versions of what we think of as jealousy.

Is jealousy an intrinsic part of human nature? Some folks say yes, some no. We say it doesn't matter. We feel what we feel—but there is a difference between jealous *feelings* and jealous *actions*. Regardless of the origin of jealous feelings, the actions we take are our responsibility.

Jealous *feelings* come from a sense of loss, or a fear of it. Jealous *actions* are usually attempts to take back control over the things we're afraid of. For example, if you feel jealous when your partner has sex with her new partner in the Monkey with Lotus Blossom and Chainsaw position, you might be afraid that you're losing something special: "That's our position! What if this new person handles the chainsaw better than I do? What does she need me for, now that she's found someone else to do this with?"

The jealous *action* might be to say, "I don't want you to have sex with anyone but me in this position," which is an attempt to deal with the fear by taking back control. "If she stops doing this, I won't feel replaced anymore!" At least until the next threatening thing comes along.

Those kinds of actions don't create safety or security. Rather, safety and security come from knowing that your partner loves, trusts and values you. Putting controls on your partner's behavior, or other jealous maneuvers like invading privacy or criticizing a metamour, won't give you this knowledge. They do exactly the opposite—they undermine intimacy by telling your partner that you don't trust *her*.

THE CHAMELEON EMOTION

Sometimes jealousy can be a relatively simple emotion, easy to detect and recognize. This is especially true when it happens in response to clear triggers, like watching a partner kiss another partner. The first time Eve saw her husband, Peter, holding hands with his first poly girlfriend, Clio, the lurching feeling of the ground dropping out from beneath her feet was an unmistakable sign of jealousy. It was impossible to interpret as anything else, and the stimulus responsible for it was clear. That made the feeling, as scary as it was, relatively straightforward to confront.

But one of the things that can make jealousy such a challenge is that it's a shape-shifter: jealousy masquerades as other emotions. Before you can fight it, you need to see it for what it is. Some of the emotions that can have jealousy at their root are fear, loneliness, loss, sadness, anger, betrayal, envy and humiliation. If you are feeling these in connection to one of your partners or metamours (your partners' other partners) and there's no obvious reason, or if the emotion is much stronger than the situation would seem to warrant, ask yourself if it might be jealousy.

On the other hand, those same emotions can arise in response to a genuinely hurtful external situation. In those cases it can be too *easy* to blame jealousy, and thereby duck the real issues. It's reasonable to ask yourself, "Am I really having these emotions just because I'm feeling jealous?" Take heed if a partner or metamour frequently minimizes your emotions as "just jealousy." Do you feel you are being listened to? Are you being offered genuine insight about yourself by someone who knows and cares about you? Or are you being belittled and dismissed?

Jealousy can be a valuable signal that we have some soul-searching to do. Managing jealousy means having enough insight to tell it apart from its imposter emotions (and vice versa) as well as from external problems that may be developing. Distinguishing it from its look-alikes means knowing yourself and communicating with your partners.

TRIGGERS FOR JEALOUSY

Sometimes jealousy is triggered by public behavior we often associate with "couplehood": holding hands in public, sending flowers to a partner's workplace, meeting a partner's parents. These triggers usually happen when we fear losing the social status that comes from being part of a couple. In polyamorous relationships, such a loss is probably inevitable: polyamory by definition expands the idea of relationships beyond the couple. These triggers can often be avoided by using the strategies we talk about in the mono/poly chapter of *More Than Two*, such as including everyone in a family portrait. It also helps to demonstrate that you are not a victim or a pawn, but a full participant in the poly relationship. For example, if you're feeling jealous about your partner's new sweetie meeting his parents, scheduling the meeting when you can also be there will show his parents that it's not happening behind your back.

A common trigger for jealousy is seeing your partner being physically affectionate or flirty with someone else. This can bring up fears of being replaced, or activate the "Why am I not enough?" script. It can also lead to destructive comparisons with your partner's other partner: "Is she sexier than I am? Prettier? Smarter? Better?"

Physical evidence of intimacy between your partner and another lover, like a condom wrapper in the trash or extra slippers at the foot of the bed, can trigger jealous feelings. So can seeing your partner do something for the first time with a new lover. Sometimes all it takes to deal with these triggers is to recognize the feelings for what they are and say, "I am feeling jealous because it seems like I'm learning to understand I'm not your only partner. Please bear with me while I work through this." Sometimes handling these triggers is more complicated, and we talk about more strategies in a bit.

LISTENING TO JEALOUSY

People often think of jealousy as evil. It can certainly make people do evil things, but by itself, jealousy is morally neutral. Like all emotions, it is the way the ancient parts of our brains—the parts that don't have language—try to communicate with us.

The problem is that as communicators go, jealousy is pretty inarticulate. It might be pointing to a significant problem in a relationship. Or it might just be our inner wordless three-year-old stomping its foot and saying "I'm not getting everything I want!" It might also be a symptom of a weak spot within us—some insecurity or self-doubt we're trying to protect. We have to decode the message if we are to decide what to do about it.

We can be tempted to approach jealousy by blaming whatever triggered it. "It's so simple! Just stop holding hands with your other partner in front of me!"

FRANKLIN'S STORY Ruby was smart, beautiful, strong, outgoing, opinionated—just the sort of person I find irresistible—and one of my first partners during my 18-year-long relationship with Celeste, my now ex-wife.

I was just out of school, and up to that point, I'd never experienced jealousy. I'd had partners who had other partners, and I'd never had even a twinge of bad feeling about it. I naively (and somewhat arrogantly) believed I was immune to jealousy—that it was something other people experienced, but not me.

I was utterly smitten with Ruby. Our relationship was emotional wildfire. Unfortunately, the terms of my agreement with Celeste didn't really permit a close, bonded relationship—which was exactly the kind of relationship Ruby and I were emotionally drawn into. We both chafed under the restrictions: no overnight stays, no public affection, a strict ceiling on how far the relationship would ever be allowed to grow. We both understood at some level that our relationship would never be permitted to become what we both needed it to be.

Before long, Ruby started another relationship with a close friend of mine, Newton. He was an excellent choice as a partner for her: quick-witted, laid-back, good-natured. His relationship with Ruby had no ceiling and no restrictions. Instinctively, I knew Newton could offer Ruby more than I could, and I was terrified that he would replace me in her heart.

The jealousy happened so fast and hit me so hard I couldn't even recognize it for what it was. All I knew was when I saw them together, I felt scared and angry. I assumed that because I felt this way, she must be doing something wrong, though it was difficult to figure out exactly what. I remember going to sleep replaying all my interactions with her in my head, looking for that thing she was doing to hurt me so much.

Because I was starting from the premise that she was doing something wrong—why else would I be feeling so bad?—I lashed out at her, accusing her of all kinds of wrongdoing, most of which existed only in my head. The tiniest, most trivial things she said or did that I didn't agree with were magnified to epic proportions. Before long, unsurprisingly, I had destroyed my relationship with Ruby, and not long after that, my friendship with her (and with Newton) as well. Not until years later did I finally put together what had happened.

By the time I realized I had been jealous, and that I had allowed my jealousy to poison my relationship with Ruby, it was far too late. I had done so much damage that neither Ruby nor Newton ever spoke to me again. I lost a partner and two friends.

Franklin destroyed his relationship with Ruby because he was unable to conceive that he might feel jealousy, and therefore he was unable to listen to it. In this case, the jealousy was saying, "You are encumbered by rules and constraints specifically intended to prevent you from having the kind of relationship both of you need. Newton is able to offer her a relationship without limits. If she wants that kind of relationship, you might be replaced."

Was Franklin actually in danger of being replaced? No. Ruby loved him very much.

How might listening to the jealousy have changed the outcome? For one, Franklin might have seen how destructive the agreements he'd made with Celeste were, and this might have saved many other people—and Franklin and Celeste—a great deal of pain. More to the point, he might have been able to go to Ruby and say, "I'm feeling jealous. I realize that our relationship is constricted, and Newton does not have these limitations. Do you still value our relationship, even as circumscribed as it is? What do I offer you, and what do you value in me? How can we make sure we build a foundation that means you will continue to want to be with me?" The outcome would probably have been very different.

It's so easy to pin responsibility for our emotions on other people. "You're making me feel this terrible thing. Stop doing that!" We forget that our emotions might be the result of our own insecurities rather than our partners' actions. When we transfer responsibility for our emotions to others, we yield control over our own lives. And when we feel that we have lost control of our own lives, we often try to take it back by controlling others.

ACCEPTING JEALOUSY

It's okay to feel jealous. That might sound strange, coming from people who are writing about polyamory. But we've been there. Almost everyone you meet has been there. Being immune to jealousy is not a prerequisite for polyamory, and feeling jealous doesn't make you a bad poly person. So take a deep breath. Like all feelings, jealousy is not the sum of who you are. It won't kill you, even if it feels like it might. It doesn't necessarily mean something's wrong with you, or with your relationship.

Even when you're feeling jealous, you still have power over your actions. Jealousy is like that creepy guy sitting behind the king whispering in his ear, "The ambassador has just insulted you most grievously, Your Grace! Attack his lands at once! Raze his villages!" But remember, you're still the king. You don't have to set the world on fire and run off to live in a cave, no matter how satisfying that sounds.

FRANKLIN'S STORY About the time I was involved with Ruby, I had a friend who had a pet iguana, a huge green lizard more than four feet long. It was usually docile and friendly. But a pattern would play out every time she took it out of its cage. She would open the door and reach inside, and it would lash at her with its whip-like tail. She would jump back, then reach into the cage again. The second time, the iguana would calmly climb up her arm to sit on her shoulder.

One day, as I watched her go through this ritual, she said, "I wish it would hit me with its tail, just once, so I wouldn't have to be afraid of it anymore."

In the aftermath of my relationship with Ruby, I was heartbroken. I spent long nights thinking about what had happened and wondering where our relationship, which had been such a source of joy to both of us, had gone so horribly wrong.

Eventually, I realized an inescapable truth: Our relationship had been destroyed because *I destroyed it*. It wasn't destroyed by her new relationship with Newton. It wasn't destroyed by anything she had done to me. I had destroyed it, because I had felt something I believed myself incapable of feeling and therefore couldn't handle when I did. She had been absolutely right to end the relationship with me. In the blindness of my own pain, I had been completely unaware of the pain I was causing her.

The things I felt during and after my relationship with Ruby were the worst I had ever felt in my life, and I didn't ever want to feel them again. And, gradually, I realized something else: *I didn't have to.* The secret of not ever feeling this way again was right in front of me. It had been all along.

First, after she broke up with me, I learned something valuable: I could lose someone, and I might want to curl up and die, but it wouldn't actually kill me. I knew what it felt like for the lizard to get me, and I didn't have to be afraid of it anymore. I would survive. I could even, eventually, be happy again.

Second, I realized she had the right to leave me. Everyone has the right to leave me. Whether they choose to leave me is something I have some control over, by the way I treat them. Ruby left because I did things that hurt her, and that drove her away. But it was within my power to do different things. It was not the hand of fate or the uncaring stars; it was the choices I made. If I had made different choices, if

I had made decisions that drew my partners closer rather than pushing them away, I might have had a better outcome.

The implications of this idea took a long time to sink in. When they did, I felt empowered. Breakups weren't something that just happened to me; they happened because of the choices I and my partner both made. I might feel pain again, but I knew there was something on the other side. And I didn't have to be afraid anymore: I would have a hand in what happened to me.

As Franklin's painful breakup shows, jealousy can cause us to act out in ways that make it more likely that whatever we're afraid of will come to pass. And as his subsequent epiphany demonstrates, jealousy can be confronted, dealt with, and banished back to the dark places where it slinks, powerless to damage your calm. Don't be discouraged. It might take work to get there, and some of that work might be uncomfortable.

Jealousy is not an identity. You may feel jealous, but that doesn't make you a jealous person. It's an important distinction. If you say "I am a jealous person," you may find it hard to think about letting go of jealousy; it feels like letting go of something that makes you who you are. On the other hand, if you say "I am a person who sometimes feels jealous," that gives space to your other emotions. "I am a person who sometimes feels jealous, and sometimes feels happy, and sometimes feels sad, excited, afraid, angry or confused." Such a statement reinforces to yourself that jealousy is not who you are.

MILA'S STORY When Mila fell in love with Morgan and agreed to be in a polyamorous relationship with him, she didn't really know what she was in for, but she knew it would be work. Morgan was already in a relationship with Nina when he started the relationship with Mila, and he started another new relationship not long after.

The first few months were hard for Mila. She didn't know where Morgan's relationships with her or with his other partners would end up. Morgan's commitment to Mila was solid, but her clarity on the future was not. She had never been insecure or jealous before, and she had a hard time accepting herself for feeling this way.

She didn't know when the jealousy would hit her or what would trigger it. Sometimes it was Morgan and Nina's public displays of affection, sometimes it was when they attended events as a couple. But the feelings often overwhelmed her. She was motivated to make a poly relationship work, though: not just by her feelings for Morgan and his steady support of her, but by her own disillusionment with monogamy after an ex had cheated on her, and her belief that doing the work would lead them to a healthier relationship in the long run. So she hung on. And importantly, Morgan created space for Mila to process her feelings and work on herself. He reassured her over and over that it was okay to feel what she felt, and he did not try to fix her feelings for her or rush her through them.

Remember, this too shall pass. When we are buried armpit-deep in an emotion, we can find it extraordinarily difficult to remember that emotions are transient. When we're sad, we can be hard put to remember what it's like to be happy, and when we're jealous, we can find it hard to remember what it's like not to feel that way. But there *is* another way to feel, even if we can't emotionally access it all the time.

CONFRONTING JEALOUSY

Sometimes jealousy triggers come as a complete surprise, which is why trying to prevent your partners from doing things that trigger jealousy doesn't work. The triggers and the underlying causes are often quite different, so lasting relief from jealousy involves digging beneath the triggers to the roots. One strategy for dealing with jealousy looks like this:

Step 1. Accept the feelings. When you look around at people in organized polyamorous communities, it can be easy to convince yourself that everyone else has conquered their jealousy, and that you're not a good poly person if you still feel it. That absolutely isn't true. Very few people say they've never felt it, and frankly, we suspect that those who do say that just haven't felt it *yet*. You can't deal with jealousy by wishing it away. Our emotions are what they are, and telling yourself "I shouldn't feel this!" won't work. The feelings might be overwhelming for awhile—even if you're experienced at poly. Accept that there's nothing wrong with you for feeling this way. You are completely normal.

Jealousy can present in a lot of ways: sometimes it's just a fluttery feeling of uncertainty or insecurity (what British poly people call "wibbles"). Other times it can be dramatic, manifesting as nausea, headaches, dizziness, dissociation or even full-blown anxiety attacks. Do whatever self-care you need to sooth yourself and ride out the feelings. Know that they will pass. What you are feeling right now is not all you are.

Remember, though, that no matter how awful you're feeling, you're accountable for your actions. As Franklin learned in his relationship with Ruby, things said can never be unsaid. Good outlets for releasing overwhelming negative feelings might include things like crying, screaming into a pillow, working out, or writing all those awful thoughts in a journal you never share or a letter you never send. But actions like verbal or physical assaults, damaging property, or invading privacy can seriously, often permanently, harm your relationships.

Step 2. Ask for support. During the initial crisis, it can be tremendously helpful for your partner to offer loving, reassuring touch, without judgment or an attempt to find an immediate solution. For many people, physical contact (without pressure to start processing just yet) helps calm those primal fears. If the partner you're feeling jealous about isn't available—if the jealousy happens when they're on a date, for example—you can turn to another partner, a close friend or even a pet if necessary.

Step 1 was to accept the feelings—and it's important for your support people to accept them, too. It's unfortunately all too common for poly people to subtly or overtly shame each other for feeling jealous, and this is never helpful. You're not less evolved or less spiritual, you're not (necessarily) clinging to a scarcity or ownership paradigm, and you're not "not really poly." You're a person who's having totally normal feelings.

It's often not helpful to try to do any serious emotional processing at this stage. Jealousy can make us feel threatened at a very deep, survival level, setting off panicked responses in some of the most ancient parts of our brains. Until those feelings have subsided, it can be hard to do the cognitive work that's needed for dealing with jealousy for the long term. Even if you're someone who likes to process verbally during intense emotional experiences, beware of making any long-term decisions right now.

Step 3. Separate triggers from causes. The next step is harder. It involves disassembling the jealousy to find where you are afraid and insecure. Long-lasting jealousy management can come only from strengthening the places where your self-esteem is weak.

Examine your triggers, the specific thoughts, actions, sights or events that set off an emotion. It's easy to believe that these triggers "cause" the emotion, but the truth is a bit more complicated. We might feel that wild rush of jealousy when we see our partner kiss another person, but that doesn't mean the kiss itself is the root cause. Instead, it's more accurate to say that the kiss is the switch that turns on a complicated chain of emotions that brings us nose-to-claw with some internal beast—a fear of being replaced, maybe, or a sense of territoriality. The kiss might be the trigger, but the cause is something else—some insecurity, stirred from its slumber.

This chain reaction is why restrictions on specific actions or behaviors rarely do much to alleviate jealousy. The beast still lies there, waiting for some other poke or prod to awaken it. At some point, if we are to be free of jealousy, we have to confront the monster directly. That means digging deep to uncover and deal with the internal things—the wobbles in our sense of worthiness, the little fears that try to convince us we will be abandoned.

Step 4. Understand the feelings. Feelings need to be examined to be understood, and the first step in examining them is to accept them for what they are. But that doesn't necessarily mean we have to *believe* them. We're often told to trust our intuition or go with our gut. But your feelings often lie to you. For example, if you're afraid of snakes, you might feel panic at the sight of a harmless corn snake crossing your path. The fear is genuine, but the thing it's telling you—*This snake is a threat to me*—is a lie.

Learning what our feelings are rooted in, without assuming that what they say is always true, is the place to start. Almost always, jealousy is rooted in some sort of fear: of abandonment, being replaced, losing the attention of someone you love, being alone. Jealousy isn't really about the person you feel jealous of. It's about you: your feeling that you might lose something precious. What is it saying? What's the outcome you're afraid will happen?

In fact, sometimes the underlying cause has nothing to do with your relationships at all. The trigger might be reminding you of unhealthy past relationships or of feelings of abandonment as a child, or it might be triggering mental health issues. Unfortunately, if this is the case, nothing you do within your relationship will help—although your partners can certainly support you while you deal with the true cause.

Getting to the roots of your jealousy takes time. When you feel jealous, you often want to act on it immediately—usually in destructive ways. Instead, take the time to figure out what's actually going on, what your jealousy is trying to tell you.

Step 5: Talk about it. Jealousy management relies on calming fears directly by talking about them and learning the way our partners feel about us. And by "talking about them," we don't mean what Franklin did in his relationship with Ruby when he said, "You terrible person, how could you make me feel this way?" We mean acknowledge and own the fear and ask for support to deal with it. "When you're on a date with him and you do that thing with your tongue, I feel jealous. That doesn't mean you shouldn't do it, but I sure could use some love and support."

This kind of communication is not always easy, especially when the jealousy arrives with a heaping side order of shame and doubt. Talking about it, though, can go a long way toward pulling out its fangs. One of the best ways to start addressing our fears in poly relationships is to ask our partners what they value in us…and trust that what they say is true. And if what they say doesn't stick, ask again. And listen. And keep at it until those things that make us magnificent in our partners' eyes start to sink in.

Step 6: Practice security. A particularly insidious thing about insecurity is that it tends to find—or invent—"evidence" to support itself. It sneaks up on you to whisper in your ear that you're not valued and not loved and your partner doesn't really want to be with you, even when those things aren't true. These things *feel* real. There is always the possibility that they *are* real, which we'll discuss in the final section—but very often, they are not, and accepting them at face value can destroy the very connection you're trying to protect.

Again, we become good at what we practice. When we practice convincing ourselves that our partners don't want us, don't value us and don't really want to be involved with us, we become good at believing it. When we practice convincing ourselves that we have value and worth and our partners treasure us, we become good at believing that.

And often a relationship *becomes* what we believe about it. If you believe your partner does not love you and treasure you, then you may act in destructive ways. You might become withdrawn, sullen or defensive, which will cause your relationship to suffer. If you believe you are cherished and valued, then you start to act with confidence, trust and openness—and people like that are great to be around. Your relationships will blossom.

Jealousy may feel intractable, but remember, it's just a feeling. Like any other emotion, it does not have to be the reality you live in.

WHEN YOU FEEL LEFT OUT

"How do you deal with feeling lonely and left out when your partner is off on a date with someone else?" This is a question Franklin gets often in emails. The answer is, perhaps, not intuitive: Focusing on how lonely and left out we feel is not the only way to respond to such a situation. This is more obvious when we aren't talking about polyamory. For example, what would we say to someone who says, "I feel lonely and left out for the eight hours a day my partner is at work"? We might think that was a little strange.

Our social values tell us it's okay for our partners to leave us for big chunks of time: for work, for errands, for military service, for all sorts of things. Yet we still tend to assume that if a partner is left behind for another romantic relationship, the natural response is to feel alienated and jealous.

Of course, it's not only romantic relationships that trigger these feelings. Many people feel left out when their partners go to the bar with drinking buddies or join a roller derby league. It's as if we have two classes of activities: those where we don't expect to feel left behind, such as work or school, and those where we do, such as a date or a derby night. It's as though we expect to feel left out when our partner is engaged in a social activity, but not if a partner is engaged in a more mundane task. So really, the feeling isn't about a partner doing something without us. Only certain kinds of activities, usually involving social situations, make us feel this way.

Maybe this is because being in a romantic relationship carries social status. Maybe it's because we don't mind missing out on mundane activities but don't want to miss out on enjoyable ones. A solution might be to build your own hobbies and social circles, so you don't have to rely on your partner to provide for all your social needs. Or maybe the feelings come from a sense of exclusion—if a partner is building a relationship with his fishing buddies, we are being rejected. The solution to this might be to work on your sense of self-worth.

Creating a strong sense of self-worth is a process, and there's no easy shortcut to doing it, but we talk about some approaches in Chapter 4 of *More Than Two*. Something to remember is that worthiness is not a *state* you need to attain, and there's no magic bar you need to cross before you'll be "good enough" to be poly. Worthiness, courage and compassion are stars to navigate by. They are not innate character traits, but practices you can cultivate, skills you can learn.

Worthiness is not the same as validation. A sense of self-worth comes from within, not from someone else. It can be tempting to look to the outside for validation: to look to your partner and say, "They love me, therefore I am worthy." But this *creates* fear rather than reducing it, because when we rely on outside things in order to feel worthy, we fear losing them all the more. We can't wait for outside evidence that we are worthy: we have to start by taking that leap of faith and believing it.

Another fear closely related to the fear of being left out is the fear of playing "second fiddle." Perhaps your partner is starting a new relationship, and maybe you aren't really being left behind—but you aren't the number one focus anymore, either. This, too, isn't just a problem in polyamory. You can become second fiddle to a new child (or grandchild), to a new job, to a new hobby…hell, Franklin has seen someone whose partner became second fiddle to a pet. (It was a very cute cat, mind, but still…)

The central issue is, how much do you trust your partner? If they want to make you a priority, they will. If they don't, they won't. The type of relationship you're in doesn't matter. Every relationship has a natural ebb and flow. Sometimes we do get supplanted, at least for a time, in our partner's attentions. When Franklin's partner Amber started working on her master's thesis, Franklin lost some of her focus and attention. When a new baby comes along, we don't find it at all surprising when the baby becomes the center of everything. When these things happen, we trust that the time will come when we are a priority again. We understand that things happen that require more attention, and that's part of life. There is a balance; we merely need to have faith in our worth, in our partner's love for us, and in our ability to ask for the things we need to reassure ourselves that the pendulum will swing back and the balance will be restored.

KEEPING SCORE

Keeping score will drive you insane. Don't do it. If you start counting the nights (or dollars) spent together, the sexual acts engaged in, the hours on the phone, or anything else of value to compare it with what you're getting, believe us when we say that no good can come of this.

You may be temporarily reassured if you come out ahead, but in the long run, all keeping score will do is make you, your partners and their partners anxious and bitter without meeting the needs you're trying to get met.

AUDREY'S STORY Audrey is in a long-term relationship with Joseph, who is married to Jasmine, who often struggles with sharing him with Audrey. After years of struggling with Jasmine's concerns over "losing" Joseph's time, Audrey and Joseph began using a spreadsheet. For two years, they used it to track the time they spent together: what scheduled time they missed, what unscheduled time they added. It tracked hours spent and lost, and whether Joseph spent time with Audrey and Jasmine individually or together as family time. Time on the phone was logged in its own category.

Their intention was to reassure Jasmine that their relationship wasn't growing outside of her comfort zone. But it didn't help. Jasmine preferred to count only time that Joseph and Audrey added *over and above* their regularly scheduled time—a lunch, coffee date or vacation day now and then—in keeping with her fear that Joseph's relationship with Audrey was getting too big. Part of Joseph and Audrey's intent in using the spreadsheet was to also show the subtractions—dates that were missed. They wanted to show that, despite Jasmine's fears that they were "growing," when you did both the addition *and* subtraction, they were actually staying "small."

However, the spreadsheet did not assuage Jasmine's fears. Joseph and Audrey are no longer keeping the spreadsheet—but Jasmine is still counting time.

If someone is keeping score, it's usually because they're afraid of something. The problem with using a scorecard to try to assuage a fear is that it does nothing to get to the root of it. Even an "even" scorecard is unlikely to diminish the fear, as Audrey's story illustrates.

Information, by itself, almost never changes feelings. If feeling secure in your relationship is contingent on seeing a certain balance on the scorecard, then you will always be comparing your relationship with another, rather than focusing on what is meaningful in your relationship: what your partner finds of value in *you*.

Taken to its conclusion, keeping score creates a relationship where people don't state their needs: they barter for what they want, using other people as the bartering chips and objectifying them in the process.

PEOPLE ARE NOT INTERCHANGEABLE

Buried in the idea of building relationships by choice rather than by default is a powerful way to combat jealousy. All too often, our relationships *do* happen by default, along lines we don't really think much about. We find the "best" person we can (whatever "best" means) and then stick that person into the "relationship slot." Sometimes when we do this, we keep half an eye out for someone better to come along.

This approach to relationships is based on a tacit assumption that people are interchangeable. If you have a relationship with Quinn, and Jordan is hotter and richer, then you can replace Quinn with Jordan, and so you climb the ladder. This approach leads to insecurity; if Quinn knows that they can be replaced by Jordan, Quinn won't ever feel secure.

The idea that people are interchangeable is fundamentally flawed. When we value the things that make our partners who they are, no one person can ever replace another.

This is one place where that leap of faith to believe in our own worthiness really pays off. When we feel ourselves worthy of love in our own right, not for the things we do or how we look but because of who we are, we become more able to recognize our own unique irreplaceability, and the irreplaceability of our partners. When we believe ourselves to be worthy, we more easily see our partners as worthy too.

Many polyamorous people will say that comparisons are poisonous to poly relationships. "Don't compare one lover to another," they say. "If you do that, you'll breed insecurity." We'd like to suggest, perhaps counterintuitively, this is not necessarily so. Some comparisons *are* damaging. "Raj is better in bed than Franco is," for example, or perhaps "Bridget is hotter than Zoe." But there's a different kind of comparison: noticing differences in a way that helps you remain aware of what makes everyone unique. That kind of comparison, which is more about treasuring the things that make people who they are than about ranking people, is awesome, because it reminds us that people are not interchangeable, and that can go a long way toward calming the fear of being replaced.

SEPARATING REALITY FROM FALSEHOOD

Believing the best of your partner isn't always easy. And devils lurk in the details. Every now and then you may find yourself in a relationship that is genuinely unhealthy, or with a partner who really does have one foot out the door. It's especially hard to sort that out from your own insecurities and determine what is true if you don't have strong self-esteem to begin with (and unhelpfully, being in such a relationship can shatter even the most resilient self-esteem).

There are no hard-and-fast rules for distinguishing between a situation where your insecurity is whispering falsehoods to you and a situation where your jealousy is a genuine signal of a painful truth. But there are external signs to look for.

One sign is a lack of empathy or compassion for what you're feeling. A partner who brushes off your fears, or isn't willing to talk to you about your jealousy, may be telling you that they're looking to leave you for better options. If your partners want to support you, they will be willing to listen to your fears, even when they're irrational. What does your partner do when you say "Honey, I have this fear"? Do they listen with compassion? Do they empathize with your feelings, even if they think your feelings are not grounded in fact? If they have done something that hurts you, do they genuinely feel sorry for it? Are they willing to take responsibility for it and make amends?

Another sign is an attitude of entitlement in a partner. This can be a bit hard to call, because at the end of the day, your partners are independent adults, carrying their own needs and feelings, and they really *are* entitled to make their own choices. But are they willing to work with you, to hear your complaints, and to make choices that support you in the long run even if you may not get everything you want in the short run? It usually doesn't work to place long-term restrictions on your partners to avoid dealing with your own insecurities—indeed, that tends only to make the insecurities stronger. But you can certainly ask your partners to help you out, and in extreme cases, it may be reasonable to agree to some temporary, limited restrictions to give you the space you need.

What do your partners say when you ask for reassurance? If you ask for concrete reminders of how your partners love and value you, do you get them? And what does the relationship itself have to say? If you've been involved with someone for three months and they already seem restless and distracted, that might be cause for concern. And if they often make implicit or explicit threats to the relationship, they may be trying to keep you off-balance as a form of emotional blackmail—or they could be feeling insecure about the relationship themselves and are trying (in an unhealthy way) to get your attention. But if you've been for years with someone who consistently treats you with loving care, and you still wake every morning feeling that this is the day they will hopscotch out of your life, then maybe what you're feeling is more about your own insecurity than about your partner's desire to leave.

QUESTIONS TO ASK YOURSELF

The following questions are helpful to consider *before* jealousy hits, to create a sort of emergency response system for dealing with your emotions when you're not thinking rationally:

- How can I take care of myself when I feel overwhelmed by my emotions?
- What reassuring things can I ask my partner to do for me when I'm riding out a jealousy storm?
- If the specific partner I'm jealous about is unavailable to me when I start feeling jealous, to whom else can I turn for reassurance, empathy, companionship or positive touch?

The following questions can be useful to think about *after* you've experienced jealousy. When you've answered them, you can start asking yourself why you feel the way you do. For example, let's say you answer yes to the question "Am I worried that if someone 'better' comes along, my partner will realize I'm not good enough and want to replace me?" That might mean your self-esteem is not high enough for you to recognize that your partner wants to be with you because they value and cherish you; some part of you may be thinking, *Well, I'm not as good as they think I am, so I better keep them away from other people! Otherwise, they'll dump me in a heartbeat.* The antidote to those feelings is to build a sense of worthiness and understand what it is about you that your partner values.

Or say you answer yes to the question "Do I believe that if I am not my partner's only sexual partner, I am not special anymore?" The remedy there is to understand that value in a relationship comes from who you are, not from what you do, so if your partner has the same experience with another person that your partner has with you, the *feeling* of that experience is still different, because nobody else is you.

- Am I worried that if someone "better" comes along, my partner will realize I'm not good enough and want to replace me?
- Am I uncertain about the value my partner sees in me? Am I not sure why they want to be with me?
- Does the idea of my partner having another lover mean that whatever my partner sees in me will no longer be valid, or that my partner will want to choose that other lover over me?
- Do I feel that most other people are sexier, more good-looking, more worthwhile, funnier, smarter or just generally better than I am, and I am not able to compete with them?
- Do I believe that if I am not jealous, I don't really love my partner?
- Do I think that if my partner falls in love with another person, my partner will leave me for that person?
- Do I think that if my partner has sex with someone "better in bed" than I am, my partner won't want to have sex with me anymore or won't need me anymore?
- Is sex the glue that holds our relationship together? If my partner has sex with someone else, do I think the relationship will come unglued?

- Do I believe that other people are willing to do sexual things that I'm not willing to do, and therefore my partner will like having sex with them better?
- Am I afraid that if my partner has sex with someone else, my partner will start comparing me whenever we have sex?
- Am I afraid that anyone my partner has sex with will try to persuade my partner to leave me?

RESOURCES

For a deeper dive into the nuances of jealousy in specific situations, check out the *Polyamory Weekly* **podcast** archives tagged "jealousy": http://polyweekly.com/category/jealousy

Franklin also has many more **essays about jealousy and insecurity** at his website: https://www.morethantwo.com/jealousy-insecurity.html

Also check out **"Emotional Outsourcing: Why Structural Approaches to Jealousy Management Fail"** on our blog: https://www.morethantwo.com/emotional-outsourcing-why-structural-approaches-to-jealousy-fail

Perhaps the best resource we've seen on cultivating self-worth is *The Gifts of Imperfection: Let Go of Who You Think You're Supposed to Be and Embrace Who You Are*, by Brené Brown. If you struggle with low self-esteem, insecurity or feelings of unworthiness, we urge you to pick up this fantastic little book.

The book *Attached: The New Science of Adult Attachment and How It Can Help You Find—and Keep—Love*, by Amir Levine and Rachel Heller provides a useful toolkit to help develop secure behaviors in your relationships.

ACKNOWLEDGMENTS

We are grateful to Alan M. MacRobert for his substantive edit of the original version of the chapter that appeared in *More Than Two*, and to Jess Mahler for her review of and contributions to this revised piece.

ALSO WITH EVE RICKERT AND FRANKLIN VEAUX

More Than Two:
A Practical Guide to Ethical Polyamory
by Franklin Veaux and Eve Rickert
with a foreword by Janet Hardy
Thorntree Press, 2014

Polysecure:
Attachment, Trauma and Consensual Nonmonogamy
by Jessica Fern
with a foreword by Eve Rickert and Nora Samaran
Thorntree Press, 2020

A World in Us:
A Memoir of Open Marriage, Turbulent Love
and Hard-Won Wisdom
by Louisa Leontiades with Eve Rickert
illustrated by Tikva Wolf, creator of Kimchi Cuddles
with a foreword by Franklin Veaux
Thorntree Press, 2017

Black Iron: A Novel
by Franklin Veaux and Eve Rickert
Thorntree Press, 2018

www.thorntreepress.com